QUESTION TIME

EXPLORE AND DISCOVER

Human Body

Angela Wilkes

KINGFISHER

NEW YORK

Editor: Carron Brown
Designer: Rebecca Johns
DTP Manager: Nicky Studdart
Consultants: Richard Walker, Norah Granger
Indexer: Jason Hook
Production Controller: Caroline Hansell
Illustrators: Roger Stuart 4–5, 8–9, 14–15, 28–29; **Alan Hancock** 29*tr*; **Jonathan Potter/Wildlife** 26*bc*, 26*cr*, 27*l*; **Mike Saunders** 22–23*c*; **Guy Smith** 6–7, 10–11, 12–13, 16–17, 18*b*, 19*tl*, 21*tl*, 23*tl*, 24–25, 26*bl*, 27*bc*.
Cartoons: Ian Dicks
Picture Research Manager: Jane Lambert
Picture acknowledgments: 5*tr* Corbis, **7***cr* Science Photo Library/Clinical Radiology Dept., Salisbury District Hospital; **13***tr* Science Photo Library/Princess Margaret Rose Orthopaedic Hospital; **15***tc* gettyone/Stone/Frank Siteman; **17***cr* Corbis; **19***cr* Science Photo Library/Mark Clarke; **21***cr* Corbis; **23***c* Corbis; **27***cr* Corbis.

Every effort has been made to trace the copyright holders of the photographs. The publishers apologize for any inconvenience caused.

KINGFISHER
Larousse Kingfisher Chambers Inc.
80 Maiden Lane
New York, New York 10038
www.kingfisherpub.com

First published in 2001
10 9 8 7 6 5 4 3 2 1

1TR/0401/TIM/RNB/NA128

LIBRARY OF CONGRESS CATALOGING–IN–PUBLICATION DATA has been applied for.

ISBN 0-7534-5341-X (HC)
ISBN 0-7534-5412-2 (PB)

Printed in China

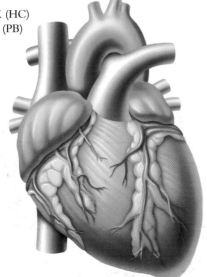

CONTENTS

4 WHY do we look different?

6 WHAT is inside your body?

8 WHY is skin different colors?

10 WHAT does your brain do?

12 WHY do you have bones?

14 WHAT makes you move?

16 HOW does blood flow?

18 HOW do you breathe?

20 HOW do you see?

22 HOW do you hear?

24 WHY do you need to eat?

26 WHERE do babies come from?

28 WHY can't babies walk and talk?

30 HUMAN BODY QUIZ

31 GLOSSARY

32 INDEX

ABOUT this book

Have you ever wondered what makes you blink? On every page, find out the answers to questions like this, and learn other fascinating facts about the human body. Words in **bold** are explained in the glossary on page 31.

Look and find ★ ★ sweat gland

All through the book you will see the **Look and find** symbol. This has the name and a picture of a small object that is hidden somewhere on the page. Look carefully to see if you can find it.

Now I know . . .

★ These boxes contain quick answers to all of the questions.
★ They will help you remember all about the amazing human body.

WHY do we look different?

People around the world are many different shapes and sizes. They may be short or tall, thin or plump. The color of their skin and hair can range from very fair to very dark. A person's appearance depends on their age, sex, and what other members of their family look like. It may even be affected by the work they do. But beneath the skin everyone's body works exactly the same way.

Head

Chest

Arm

Abdomen

Leg

WHAT are the main parts of the body?

All bodies are made of the same basic parts. Your head is at the top of your body. The trunk of your body has two parts: the chest in the upper half and the **abdomen** in the lower half. Your two arms and two legs make up your four limbs.

That's amazing!

No two fingerprints are the same!

Babies cannot talk, so they cry to let people know they want something!

HOW do you communicate?

People communicate mainly by talking and listening to each other. You have a voice that your family and friends know at once, but you can communicate in other ways too. When people talk to you, they look at your face. This is because your smile and other facial expressions show what you are feeling. You also use body language, such as pointing and waving.

People who are hearing impaired have difficulty hearing. They may communicate with sign language, using hand signs and facial expressions for certain words.

Now I know . . .

★ People all look different, but their bodies work the same way.
★ All bodies are made up of a head, chest, abdomen, and limbs.
★ You communicate mainly by talking and listening.

5

WHAT is inside your body?

Your body is like a piece of machinery. It is made up of thousands of different parts all tightly packed together beneath your skin. Important body parts, such as **muscles**, bones, and other **organs**, are controlled by **nerves** and supplied by blood vessels that carry blood to them. These hidden parts of your body work nonstop, day and night to keep you alive, give you energy, and make you grow.

HOW does your body work?

Inside your body there are several different systems that work alongside each other. Each system is made up of a group of organs. These are all joined together to carry out important jobs, such as carrying **oxygen**, moving bones, or **digesting** food. The different systems all work together smoothly to keep your body working properly.

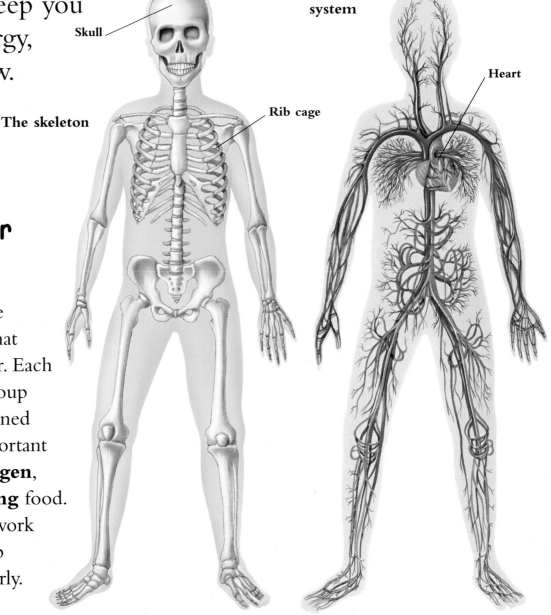

The blood system

Skull

The skeleton

Rib cage

Heart

That's amazing!

It is always warm inside you—in fact, your body stays at a temperature of about 98.6°F (37°C)!

About two thirds of your body is made of water!

WHERE are your main organs?

Most of your body's main organs are inside your head, chest, and abdomen. Your liver is in the upper abdomen. Close by are two kidneys, one on either side of your spine. Bones protect many of the organs from damage. Your brain is hidden inside your skull, which forms your head. In your chest, your heart and lungs are protected by your rib cage.

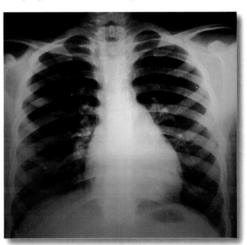

This **X ray** of a chest shows the heart (in the middle) and lungs (the dark areas at either side of the heart) inside the rib cage.

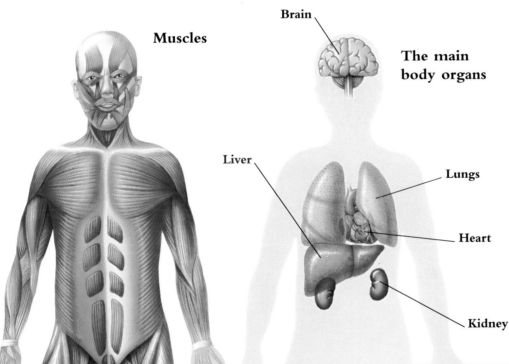

Muscles

Brain

The main body organs

Liver

Lungs

Heart

Kidney

Now I know . . .

★ There are thousands of different body parts beneath your skin.
★ Several body systems work together inside you.
★ Your main organs are deep inside you, protected by bones.

7

Look and find ★ ★ *sweat gland*

WHY is skin different colors?

Your skin covers your whole body. It is stretchy and fits you like a glove. Some people have pale skin, and others have dark skin. This is because skin has brown coloring in it called melanin. If your skin has a lot of melanin, you will have darker skin than someone whose skin has a small amount. Melanin protects your body from the sun's harmful rays. If you spend a lot of time in the sun, your skin makes more melanin, and you get a suntan.

WHAT makes people sweat?

Sweating helps you stay at the same temperature. Deep in your skin coiled tubes called sweat glands make watery sweat. Beads of sweat rise to the surface of your skin through tiny holes called **pores**. The sweat **evaporates**, and this helps cool you down.

When you exercise, you get hot, and this makes you sweat.

Everyone needs to wear suntan lotion to stop the sun's rays from burning their skin.

HOW do you feel pain?

Your skin gives you your sense of touch. Beneath its extremely thin surface there is a layer called the **dermis**. This is packed with tiny nerve endings that send messages to your brain when you touch things. Some nerve endings react to pressure, movement, or heat and cold; others detect pain. The dermis contains oil glands that make oils to keep your skin soft. It also has hair follicles—tiny holes in your skin from which your hairs grow.

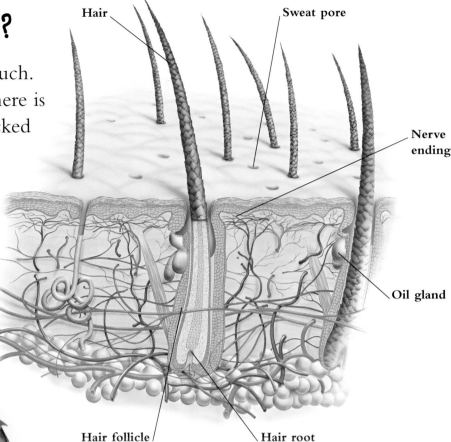

Hair

Sweat pore

Nerve ending

Oil gland

Hair follicle

Hair root

That's amazing!

If you didn't have skin, your insides would dry out like a raisin!

You lose and replace about 90 hairs a day!

Now I know . . .

★ Skin has brown coloring in it called melanin, which gives your skin color.
★ Skin makes watery sweat to help your body cool down.
★ Skin contains nerve endings that give you your sense of touch.

WHAT does your brain do?

Your brain is an organ inside your skull that is about as big as your two fists. Yet it does far more than any computer and controls your whole body. It is where you think, have feelings and ideas, learn things, and store memories. It also keeps every part of your body working. The brain is divided into many different areas, each of which controls the different things you do, say, think, feel, and see.

The nervous system

Spinal cord

Sight area

HOW is your brain joined to the rest of your body?

Your brain is made of billions of connected nerve **cells**. It is joined to the rest of your body by the spinal cord—a long bundle of nerves that runs down the center of your spine. Nerves are like wires, carrying tiny electrical signals that flash to the brain and back again. They branch out from the spinal cord to every part of your body. Your brain and nerves make up your nervous system.

Balance area

Hearing area

10

The right half
of the brain

Touch area

Movement
area

Any one cell in your brain may be connected
to as many as 10,000 other brain cells!

Signals flash between the brain and nerves at
speeds of up to 250 mph (400km/h)!

WHY doesn't your body stop working when you go to sleep?

Your brain works automatically
day and night, so your body keeps
working even when you are fast
asleep. The brain stem at the base
of your brain joins your brain to the
spinal cord. It controls many things
without you having to think about
them, such as how fast your heart
beats and how often you breathe.

Thinking,
personality,
and emotions
area (front of
your brain)

Talking area
(usually on the left
half of your brain)

Now I know . . .

★ The brain is the control center
   for your entire body.
★ Your brain is joined to your body
   by the spinal cord and nerves.
★ Your brain works automatically
   day and night.

11

WHY do you have bones?

There are more than 206 bones inside you. All together, they make up your skeleton. Your skeleton gives your body support and shape—without it you would collapse in a heap. Bones are different sizes and shapes, depending on the weight they support and the work they do. Your thighbones are the largest bones in your body. They are long and strong to support the weight of your body whenever you stand up, run, walk, or jump.

HOW do bones fit together?

Most of your bones are connected by joints, so they can move in different directions. The knee joint is where the curved bottom end of the thighbone fits into the curved top end of the shinbone. The ends of the bones are covered in a slippery fluid so your knee can move back and forth smoothly.

That's amazing!

Nearly half the bones in your body are in your hands, feet, wrists, and ankles!

You have exactly the same number of neck bones as a giraffe!

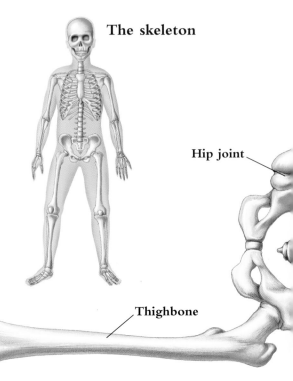

The skeleton

Hip joint

Knee joint

Kneecap

Ankle joint

Shinbone

Thighbone

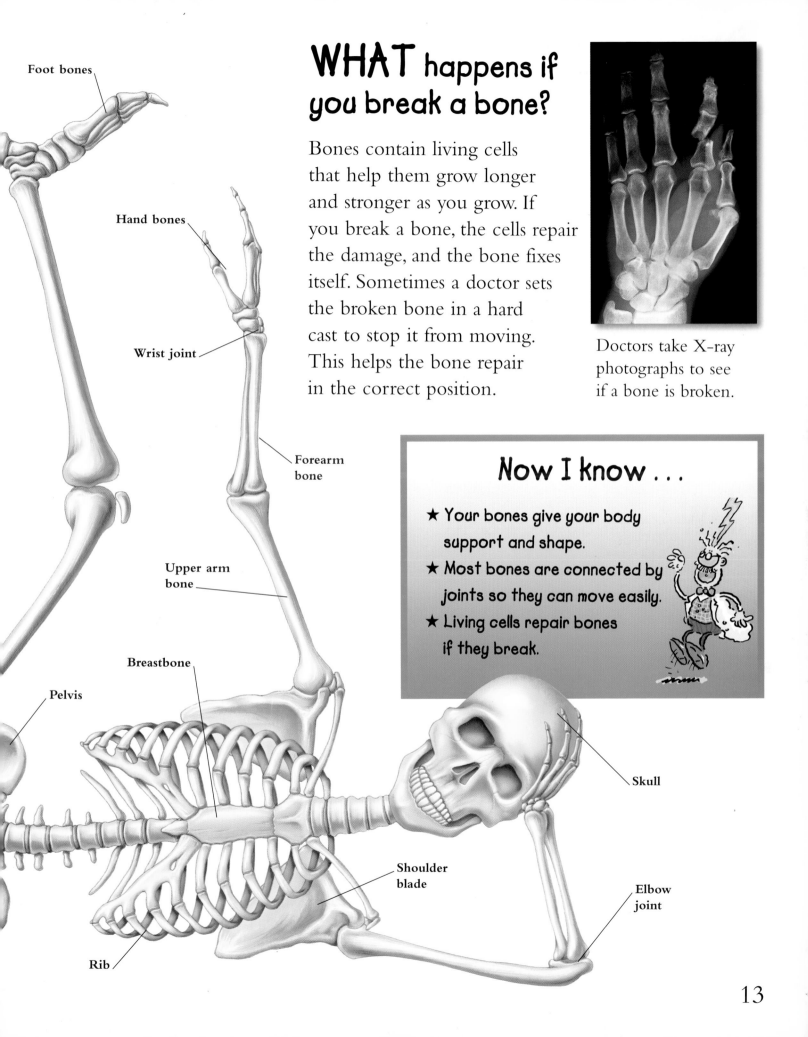

Foot bones

Hand bones

Wrist joint

Forearm
bone

Upper arm
bone

Breastbone

Pelvis

Rib

WHAT happens if you break a bone?

Bones contain living cells that help them grow longer and stronger as you grow. If you break a bone, the cells repair the damage, and the bone fixes itself. Sometimes a doctor sets the broken bone in a hard cast to stop it from moving. This helps the bone repair in the correct position.

Doctors take X-ray photographs to see if a bone is broken.

Now I know . . .

★ Your bones give your body support and shape.

★ Most bones are connected by joints so they can move easily.

★ Living cells repair bones if they break.

Shoulder
blade

Skull

Elbow
joint

WHAT makes you move?

Every movement you make, from a blink to a jump, is made by muscles. You have over 600 different muscles. Many of them are attached to your bones by strong, ropelike bands called tendons, which allow you to move every part of your body. There are also muscles in your skin and eyes, and others that keep your heart pumping and your insides working without you having to think about them.

HOW do muscles work?

When you tighten a muscle, it gets shorter and thicker and pulls on whatever it is attached to. Most muscles work in pairs. For example, you tighten the biceps muscle to bend your arm. To straighten your arm, the triceps muscle tightens and the biceps muscle relaxes.

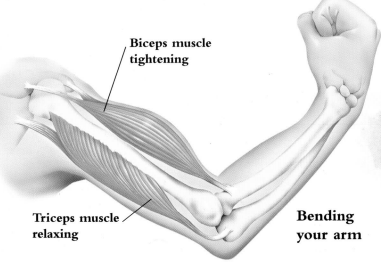

Biceps muscle tightening

Triceps muscle relaxing

Bending your arm

14

WHY do dancers need to warm up?

For muscles to work well they need a good supply of blood and oxygen. Dancers and athletes do gentle exercises to loosen and stretch

their muscles before they start any exercise. This increases the blood flow to their muscles, giving them more energy. If you exercise hard without warming up, you risk getting painful cramps, or you may strain and injure your muscles.

That's amazing!

Nearly half of your body weight is made up of muscles!

You use eight to twelve different muscles in your face just to smile!

Now I know . . .

★ Every movement of your body is made by muscles.
★ Muscles work by pulling on parts of the body.
★ Dancers warm up to increase the blood flow to their muscles.

HOW does blood flow?

Blood flows around your body all the time, carrying oxygen and food to every cell and taking away **waste**. Your blood is pumped throughout your body by your heart, an organ with strong walls made of muscle. First the blood is sent to your lungs to get oxygen, then it returns to your heart and is pumped to the rest of your body. The tubes that carry blood away from the heart are called **arteries**. Those that carry blood back to the heart are called **veins**.

Vein carrying blood from the upper body

WHAT is blood made of?

More than half of your blood is made of a pale liquid called plasma. Floating in it are red cells, white cells, and platelets. Billions of saucer-shaped red cells carry oxygen around your body. Different types of white cells fight **germs** to protect your body from infection. Tiny platelets help your blood to clot and form a scab if you cut yourself and bleed.

Vein carrying blood from the lower body

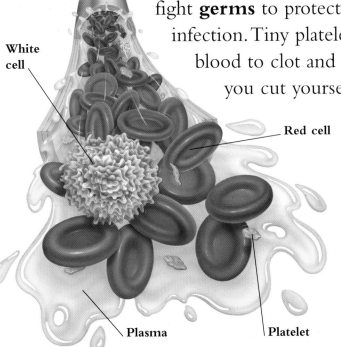

White cell

Red cell

Plasma

Platelet

That's amazing!

Your heart beats about 100,000 times a day, every day of your life, without getting tired!

An adult's heart pumps a staggering 4,000 gallons (15,000l) of blood a day!

16

Artery carrying
blood to the body

Artery
carrying
blood to
the lungs

WHY does your heart sometimes beat fast?

When you bicycle or do any other exercise, your muscles need extra oxygen to give you more energy. Your brain sends signals to your heart, which beats harder and faster to pump more blood to your muscles. You also breathe faster to take in more oxygen, so there is more oxygen in your blood.

The heart and kidneys

Heart

Kidneys remove any chemicals in your blood that your body does not need.

Arteries and veins supply the heart itself with blood.

Now I know . . .

★ Your heart pumps blood around your body nonstop.
★ Blood is made of plasma, red cells, white cells, and platelets.
★ Your heart beats faster when you need extra energy.

HOW do you breathe?

You breathe because your body needs oxygen, a gas, to stay alive. Your lungs are like two sponges full of tiny air tubes that branch off—like a tree—from your windpipe. When you breathe in, your lungs swell up as air fills the tubes. Oxygen passes out of the tubes and into your blood to travel around your body. At the same time, a waste gas called **carbon dioxide** passes from your blood into your lungs. Your lungs shrink again as you breathe out.

WHAT does your nose do?

You breathe in air through your nose and down your windpipe to your lungs. Your nose warms the air you breathe in. **Mucus** and hairs inside your nose also trap dirt to stop it from reaching your lungs. A small area at the top of your nose is full of nerve cells that detect smells in the air. These give you your sense of smell.

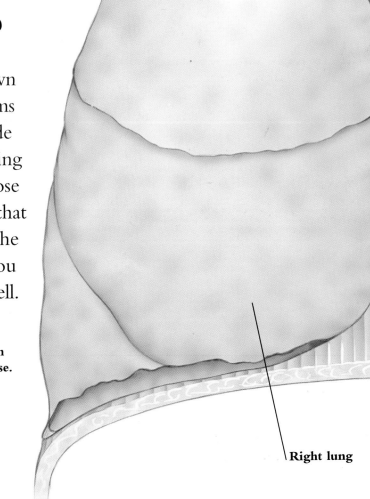

Windpipe

Right lung

Air is breathed in through your nose.

Air travels down your windpipe.

18

The lungs

Left lung is smaller than the right one to make room for your heart

That's amazing!

You take about 23,000 breaths every day!

The nerve cells in your nose can detect 10,000 different smells!

WHY do people cough?

If dust, germs, or mucus get into your windpipe or the air tubes in your lungs and irritate them, you cough automatically. You take a deep breath, and pressure builds up inside your lungs. When you cough, air shoots out of your lungs. The rush of air out of your lungs makes the **vocal cords** in your throat rattle, and you hear your cough as a noise. The cough also shoots out dust, germs, and mucus along with air.

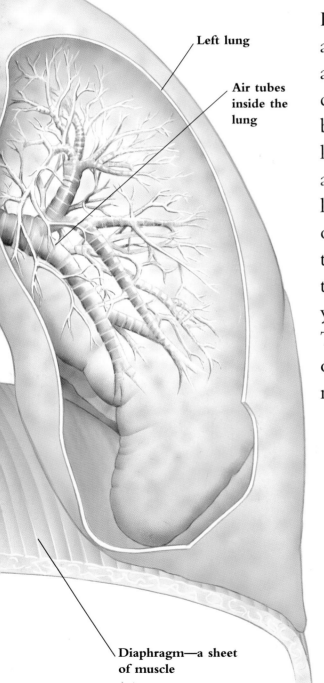

Left lung

Air tubes inside the lung

Diaphragm—a sheet of muscle

Now I know . . .

★ You breathe because your body needs oxygen to stay alive.

★ Your nose warms the air you breathe in and traps dirt.

★ People cough to get rid of dirt in their windpipe or lungs.

★ Look and find ★

lens

HOW do you see?

Your eyes pick up light that is reflected from whatever you look at. They send signals to your brain telling you what you see. The light bends as it goes through the cornea at the front of your eye. It then passes into the eye itself through a hole called the pupil. A lens focuses the light and forms moving images of what you see onto the retina, or the back wall of the eye. Millions of light-sensitive cells in the retina then send the images to your brain along the optic nerve.

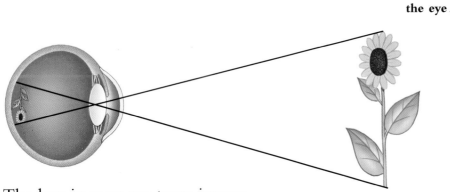

The lens in your eye turns images upside down, but your brain turns them right side up for you.

WHAT makes you blink?

You blink automatically every two to ten seconds to keep the delicate surface of each eye healthy. When your eyelids close, they spread tear fluid across your eyes to wash away dust and germs and to keep the surface moist.

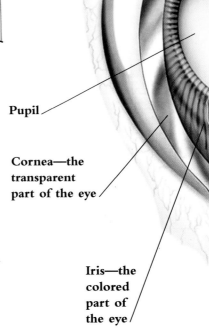

White of the eye

Pupil

Cornea—the transparent part of the eye

Iris—the colored part of the eye

Lens

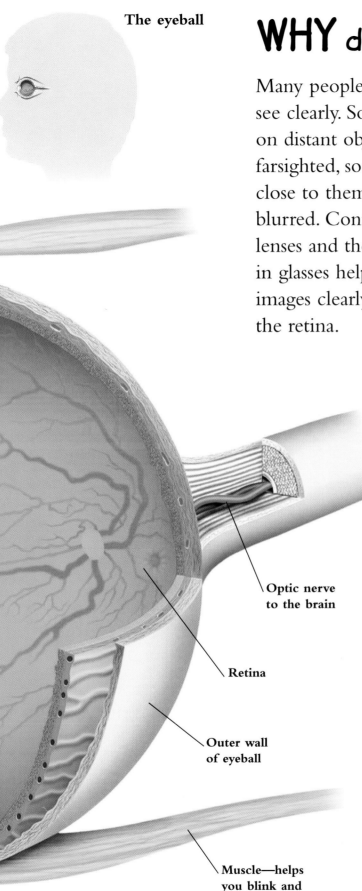

The eyeball

Optic nerve
to the brain

Retina

Outer wall
of eyeball

Muscle—helps
you blink and
swivel your eyes

WHY do some people wear glasses?

Many people need glasses or contact lenses to help them see clearly. Some people are nearsighted and cannot focus on distant objects, which look blurred. Other people are farsighted, so things close to them look blurred. Contact lenses and the lenses in glasses help focus images clearly on the retina.

That's amazing!

On average you blink about 10,000 times a day!

You have 200 eyelashes around each eye to keep out dust and dirt!

Now I know . . .

★ Your eyes and brain work together to help you see.
★ You blink to clean dust and germs out of your eyes.
★ People wear glasses so they can see clearly.

21

Look and find
★ ★
ear wax

HOW do you hear?

Sounds travel through the air as vibrations called sound waves. Your ears pick up these sound waves and send signals to your brain. The outer part of each ear carries the sound waves to your eardrum, which vibrates. These vibrations pass along tiny bones to the cochlea. This is a spiral-shaped tube full of liquid deep inside your ear. The liquid moves and triggers tiny hairs that are attached to nerve cells. These send signals to your brain, and you hear sounds.

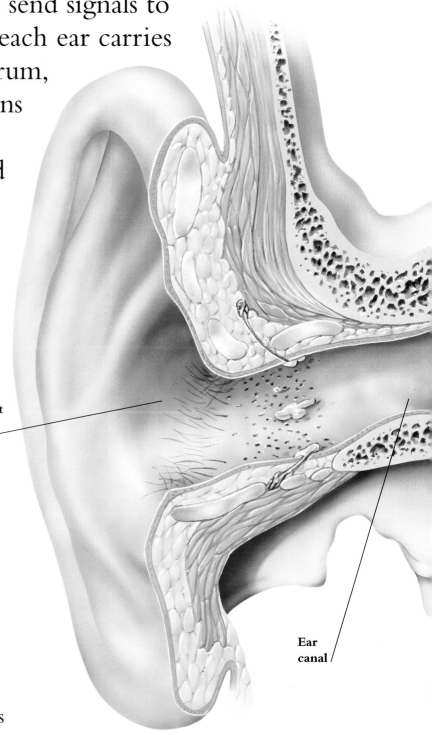

The fleshy, outer part of your ear acts as a funnel

Ear canal

WHY do you have two ears?

Having two ears helps you tell where a sound is coming from. If something makes a noise to your right, the sound waves it makes reach your right eardrum a split second before they reach your left eardrum. Your brain notices the difference in timing and helps you tell where the sound is coming from.

The right ear

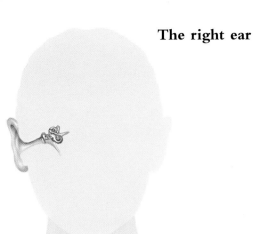

That's amazing!

You can tell the difference between over 1,500 different tones of sound!

No two people have exactly the same shaped ears!

Semicircular canals

Nerve leading to brain

Cochlea

Eardrum vibrates like skin on a drum when sound waves hit it

WHAT keeps you balanced?

Your ears help you keep your balance. Three tubes called semicircular canals are inside your ear. These contain fluid and nerve cells connected to tiny hairs. When your head moves, the fluid and hairs in the tubes move. This sends nerve signals to your brain, telling you if you are standing up.

Now I know . . .

★ Your ears pick up sound waves in the air so you can hear.
★ Having two ears helps you judge where sounds come from.
★ Your ears help you keep your balance.

WHY do you need to eat?

You cannot live without food. It gives you energy and makes you grow. Eating different foods also keeps you healthy and helps you get better if you are sick or have hurt yourself. Before your body can use the food you eat, it has to be broken down into tiny bits, so that useful pieces called **nutrients** are small enough to pass into your blood. This process is called digestion. Your digestive system starts in your mouth and is made up of several organs that break down the food as it passes through them.

WHERE does food go?

Liver—organ that removes nutrients after they have been through the small intestine

Your teeth and **saliva** break down food in your mouth. Once you have swallowed the food, it is squeezed down a tube called the esophagus to your stomach. There it is churned up and mixed with chemicals to make a thick soup. This mixture is squeezed slowly along a long, wiggly tube called the small intestine. Nutrients pass through its thin walls into your blood to go around your body. The remaining food travels to your large intestine, which soaks up water. Solid wastes are stored in your rectum until you go to the bathroom.

That's amazing!

On average a person eats 30 tons of food and drinks 13,200 gallons (50,000l) of liquid during their lifetime!

Your tongue has more than 10,000 taste buds on its surface!

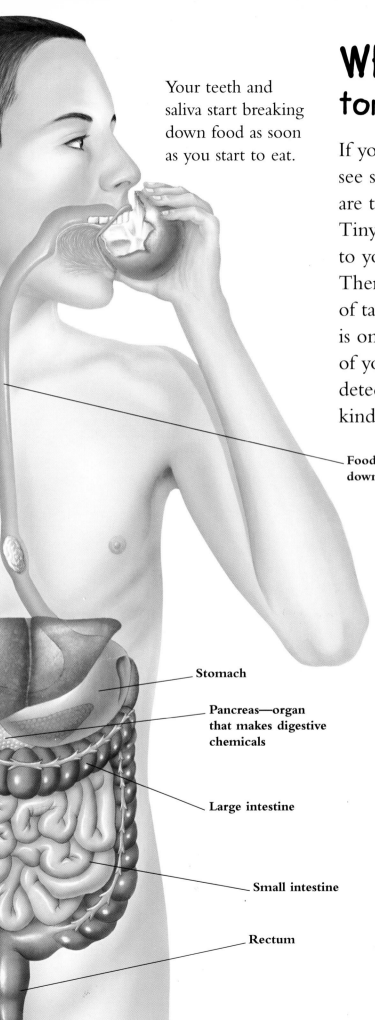

Your teeth and saliva start breaking down food as soon as you start to eat.

Food travels down esophagus

Stomach

Pancreas—organ that makes digestive chemicals

Large intestine

Small intestine

Rectum

WHY is the surface of your tongue bumpy?

If you look at your tongue in a mirror, you can see small bumps on it. Around each bump there are taste buds. These give you your sense of taste. Tiny sense cells detect flavors and send messages to your brain, which identifies them. There are four different types of taste buds. Each type is on a different part of your tongue and detects a particular kind of taste.

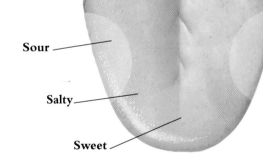

Bitter

Sour

Salty

Sweet

Now I know . . .

★ Food gives you energy, makes you grow, and keeps you healthy.
★ Food travels through organs in your digestive system.
★ The surface of your tongue is covered with bumpy taste buds.

25

WHERE do babies come from?

Women have egg cells inside them, and men have sperm cells. Both are needed to make a baby. Every baby starts life as a tiny cell smaller than a grain of salt! This cell is made when a man and woman make love. They hug, kiss, and stroke each other's bodies, and the man puts liquid full of sperm cells into the woman. If one of the sperm cells joins an egg cell inside the woman, they make a new cell that settles in the **womb** in her abdomen and starts to grow into a baby.

HOW long did you live in your mother's womb?

You lived in your mother's womb for about nine months, living in a bag of warm fluid. You could not eat or breathe by yourself. Instead, you got all your food and oxygen through a tube called the **umbilical cord**, which went from your belly button to your mother.

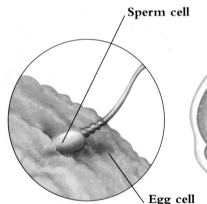

Sperm cell

Egg cell

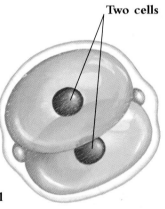

Two cells

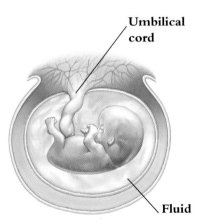

Umbilical cord

Fluid

1 Sperm look like tadpoles. When a sperm cell finds an egg cell, it wriggles into it, and they join together.

2 The egg splits into two cells. They keep dividing, making a ball of cells that grows bigger and bigger.

3 After 2 months all the main organs of the baby have formed, and it is floating in a bag of fluid.

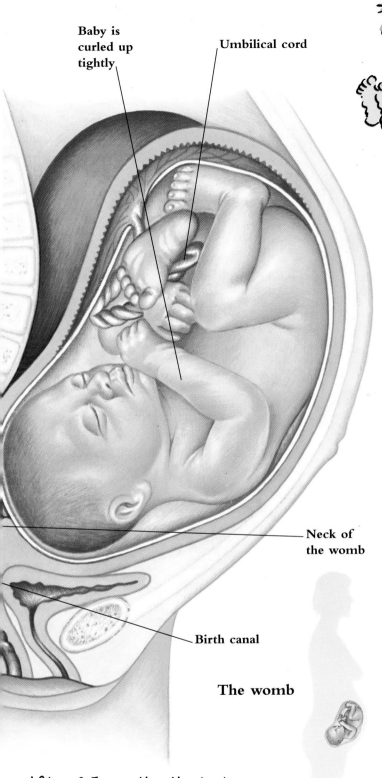

Baby is curled up tightly

Umbilical cord

Neck of the womb

Birth canal

The womb

4 After 8.5 months the baby is fully developed and is very squashed in the womb. It is usually upside down, and it is ready to be born.

That's amazing!

A baby's head is about a fourth of its total body length!

If you continued growing at the same speed as you did in the womb, you would be 6 ft. (2m) tall by your first birthday!

HOW are babies born?

The muscles in the wall of the womb are very strong. When a baby is ready to be born, these muscles tighten and push the baby down. The neck of the womb slowly opens until it is big enough for the baby's head to go through. The mother's muscles squeeze harder and slowly push the baby along the birth canal and out of her body.

Now I know . . .

★ A baby starts to grow when a man's sperm cell joins a woman's egg cell.
★ You lived in your mother's womb for about nine months.
★ A baby is born when its mother's womb muscles push it out.

WHY can't babies walk and talk?

Babies' muscles are not very strong, and they cannot control them very well. They can kick their legs and make sounds, but they do not know how to stand up or talk yet. Babies have to find out what their bodies can do and learn all the basic skills they need for life.

They do this by copying other people and trying things out again and again. As you grow up you spend a lot of time trying out and learning new skills, even when you are playing.

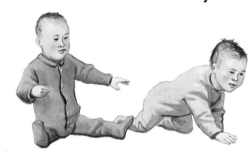

One-year-olds have big heads compared to their bodies, and short arms and legs.

Six-year-olds are much taller. Their bodies are longer compared to their heads.

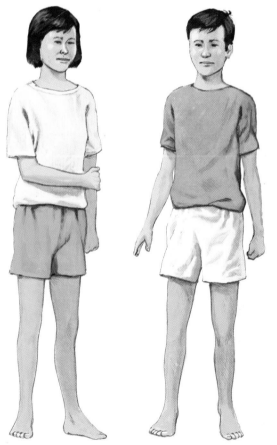

At 14, people have longer arms and legs. Their bodies look more like adult bodies.

At 20, people are adults. Their bodies are fully grown and developed.

HOW do you grow?

When you are a child, your bones grow fast, changing what you look like. They do not grow at the same time. When you were an infant, your brain was large compared to the rest of you, so the top of your skull was big, and your face was small. As you grow older your skull grows a little, but your face bones grow more.

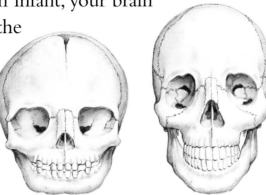

Six-year-old's skull   **16-year-old's skull**

That's amazing!

Most children recognize 200 words by the time they are two years old!

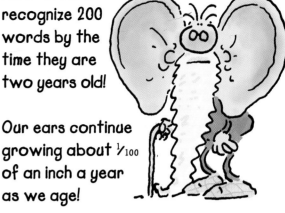

Our ears continue growing about $\frac{1}{100}$ of an inch a year as we age!

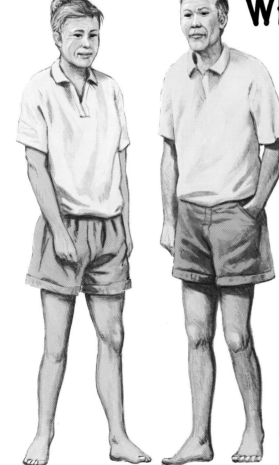

At 60, people are usually slightly smaller, with smaller muscles, gray hair, and wrinkled skin.

WHEN do you stop growing?

Babies grow very fast. By the time they are one year old, they grow more slowly. Different parts of the human body grow at different times, so it changes shape as it grows. Teenagers have a growth spurt, and they suddenly grow very fast for a short time. Most people stop growing between the ages of 18 and 20.

Now I know . . .

★ Babies learn how to control their muscles in order to walk and talk.
★ People continue growing until they are 18 to 20 years old.
★ You grow because the bones inside you are growing.

HUMAN BODY QUIZ

What have you remembered about the human body? Test what you know and see how much you have learned.

1 What protects your heart and lungs?
a) Your spine
b) Your rib cage
c) Your muscles

2 Which part of your body contains melanin?
a) Your brain
b) Your lungs
c) Your skin

3 What carries messages to and from your brain?
a) Nerves
b) Muscles
c) Bones

4 What make up your skeleton?
a) Bones
b) Joints
c) Muscles

5 What happens when you tighten a muscle?
a) It gets longer
b) It gets shorter
c) It relaxes

6 What carries oxygen around your body?
a) Nerves
b) Blood
c) Food

7 What is the colored part of your eye called?
a) The lens
b) The pupil
c) The iris

8 Where in your body can you find the cochlea?
a) In your ear
b) In your eye
c) In your brain

9 What goes from your mouth to your stomach?
a) Your small intestine
b) Your windpipe
c) Your esophagus

10 Where does a baby grow inside a woman?
a) Her womb
b) Her stomach
c) Her chest

Find the answers on page 32.

GLOSSARY

abdomen The lower half of the trunk of your body that contains your kidneys and digestive organs.

arteries Tubes that carry blood from your heart to other parts of your body. The blood they carry is usually full of oxygen.

carbon dioxide A waste gas in the air that your body releases when you breathe out.

cells The tiny living things that make up your body.

dermis The layer in your skin that contains sweat glands, nerves, and arteries.

digesting Breaking down food into tiny pieces that your body can use.

evaporates Dries up and becomes tiny drops of water vapor in the air.

germs Tiny living things that can get into your body and make you sick.

mucus Slimy liquid in your nose and throat.

muscles Parts of your body that make you move.

nerves Wirelike parts in your body that carry messages to and from the brain and spinal cord.

nutrients Useful parts of food that your body needs for growth, energy, and health.

organs Important parts of the body that carry out different functions.

oxygen A gas in the air; you need to breathe it in to live.

pores Tiny holes in your skin.

saliva Spit inside your mouth that contains a chemical that breaks down food.

umbilical cord The tube that joins an unborn baby to its mother's womb.

veins Tubes that carry blood back to your heart. The blood they carry is usually low in oxygen.

vocal cords Two stretchy flaps in your throat that vibrate and make sounds when air passes through them.

waste Leftover food, fluids, gases, or chemicals that your body does not need and must get rid of.

womb An organ in a woman's abdomen where an unborn baby grows.

X ray A type of photograph that shows solid things, such as bones, inside your body.

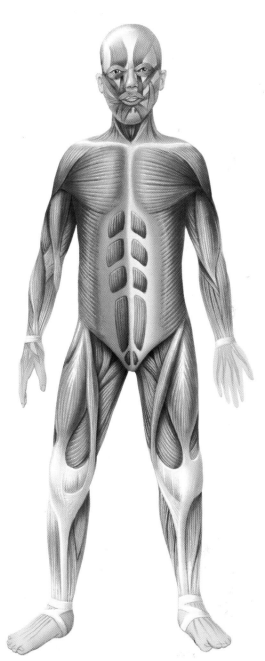

INDEX

eating 24–25, 26
emotions 10, 11
energy 6, 15, 17, 24, 25
exercise 15, 17
eyes 14, 20–21, 28

A

abdomen 4, 5, 7, 31
appearance 4
arms 4, 13, 14, 28
arteries 16, 17, 31

B

babies 4, 26, 27, 28, 29
balance 10, 23
birth 27
blinking 14, 20, 21
blood 6, 15, 16–17, 18, 24
bones 6, 7, 12–13, 22, 29
brain 7, 9, 10–11, 17, 20,
    21, 22, 23, 25, 29
breathing 11, 17, 18, 19, 26

C

carbon dioxide 18, 31
cells 10, 11, 13, 16, 17, 18,
    19, 20, 22, 23, 25, 26, 27, 31
coughing 19

D

digestive system 24, 25

E

ears 4, 22–23, 29

F

fingerprints 4
food 6, 16, 24–25, 26

G

germs 16, 19, 20, 21, 31
glasses 21
growing 6, 13, 24, 25, 27,
    28, 29

H

hair 4, 9, 18, 22, 23, 29
hands 5, 12, 13, 26
head 4, 5, 23, 27, 28, 29
health 13, 15, 16, 19, 24, 25
hearing 5, 10, 22, 23
heart 6, 7, 11, 14, 16, 17, 19

I

intestines 24–25

J

joints 12, 13

K

kidneys 7, 17

L

learning 10, 28, 29
legs 4, 12, 28
liver 7, 24
lungs 7, 16, 17, 18–19

M

melanin 8, 9
mucus 18, 19, 31
muscles 6, 7, 14, 15, 16,
    17, 21, 27, 28, 29, 31

N

nerves 6, 9, 10, 11, 18, 19,
    20, 21, 22, 23, 31
nervous system 10
nose 18, 19
nutrients 24, 31

O

organs 6, 7, 10, 16, 24, 25,
    31
oxygen 6, 15, 16, 17,
    18–19, 26, 31

R

rib cage 6, 7, 13

S

saliva 24, 25, 31
sight 10, 20–21
sign language 5

T

talking 4, 5, 11, 28, 29
taste 24, 25
teeth 24, 25
temperature 7, 8, 9
thinking 10, 11
tongue 24, 25
touch 9, 11

U

umbilical cord 26, 27, 31

V

veins 16, 17, 31
vocal cords 19, 31

W

windpipe 18, 19
womb 26–27, 31

X

X rays 7, 13, 31

skeleton 6, 12–13
skin 4, 6, 7, 8–9, 14, 29
skull 6, 7, 10, 13, 29
smell 18, 19
sound 22–23, 28
sweating 8, 9

Answers to the Human Body Quiz on page 30
★ 1 b ★ 2 c ★ 3 a ★ 4 a ★ 5 b ★ 6 b ★ 7 c ★ 8 a ★ 9 c ★ 10 a

32

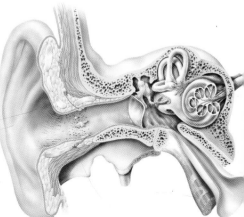